THE PSYCHOMETRIC TESTING POCKETBOOK

By Dr Barry Cripps & Dorothy Spry

Drawings by Phil Hailstone

"This Pocketbook is a good source of important and quick information presented in bite-size pieces that are both easily digestible and nourish one's basic knowledge of how, when and why to assess people in the corporate world."

Dr Reuven Bar-On, Author of the EQ-i

G000146467

Published by:
Management Pocketbooks Ltd
Laurel House, Station Approach, Alresford, Hants SO24 9JH, U.K.
Tel: +44 (0)1962 735573   Fax: +44 (0)1962 733637
E-mail: sales@pocketbook.co.uk
Website: www.pocketbook.co.uk

This edition published 2008.

British Library Cataloguing-in-Publication Data – A catalogue record for this book is available from the British Library.

ISBN 978 1 903776 43 8

Design, typesetting and graphics by **efex ltd**. Printed in U.K.

CONTENTS

 INTRODUCTION 5
Aims of pocketbook, benefits to the
organisation, definition, what makes a
good test, selecting the right one,
necessary ingredients, good practice

 TESTING FOR SELECTION 15
Why use selection tests, intelligence
testing, golden triangle, case studies
for ability tests (GAT 2), aptitude (CPAB),
critical reasoning (W-GCTA^{UK}),
personality (16PF®5) and work style
(Thomas International System PPA)

 **TESTING FOR
ORGANISATIONAL DEVELOPMENT** 47
Definitions of OD and EI, case study for
emotional intelligence (Bar-On EQ-i),
multi-rater 360 EI feedback (EQ-360),
well-being (quality of working life
questionnaire), management
development (Wave Professional Styles)

 TESTING FOR TEAMS 65
Why use team tests, case studies for
team roles (Belbin®) and team building
(Myers-Briggs Type Indicator®), high
similarity and contrasting teams

 **TESTING FOR PERSONAL
DEVELOPMENT** 85
At the crossroads, motivational tests, case
study (SHL Motivation questionnaire),
personality tests, case study (ECCOS),
EI ability case study (MSCEIT)

 **TESTING FOR CAREER
COUNSELLING** 107
Interests and values inventories, case
study (Strong Interest Inventory® (SII)
Tool and Gordon's Surveys of Personal
and Interpersonal Values)

 USEFUL INFORMATION 117
Testing online: advantages and
disadvantages, good practice,
standards in testing, conclusion,
further reading & references

FROM THE AUTHORS

The very words **psychometric** and **testing** can be enough to clear a room, and sound sufficiently alarming to prevent many people from considering using tests in the first place. In addressing this topic it is not our intention to give you a headache, or swamp you with too many scientific and statistical facts.

Instead, we are keen to introduce the non-specialist reader to the world of psychometric testing in as practical and user-friendly a way as possible. This pocketbook is written for managers in human resources, line managers, administrators and anyone who needs to know about workplace testing in all its forms. Further reading references are provided at the end of the book for individuals who wish to delve more deeply into the scientific background behind each test mentioned.

1NTRODUCTION

“ To test or not to test, that is the question…
… and then, which test to use? ”

AIM OF THIS POCKETBOOK

The aim of this pocketbook is to act as a practical guide, taking you step by step through the process of selecting the most appropriate psychometric test or tests, in order to provide your own workplace solutions.

We will start by introducing a workplace scenario, looking at what the organisation needs to achieve, and then explain how the testing can be used to bring this about. A mixture of popular psychometric tests has been selected and will be supported by a range of situational case studies for the following areas:

- Selection
- Promotion
- Managing your team and team development
- Personal development: growing potential in the individual
- Career counselling and development

This book is **not** about:

- ✗ Training you to use tests – though we do suggest ways to become fully trained

- ✗ Recommending any specific test – we do, however, demonstrate commonly used tests

- ✗ Fully reviewing any particular test – but we do show you how to obtain full test reviews

BENEFITS OF TESTING TO YOUR ORGANISATION

Some of the benefits of using a good psychometric test or tests to assess people are that they give results that are:

- Objective – not influenced by personal feelings or opinions
- Systematic – working to a fixed plan
- Reliable – able to be trusted, because they are consistent across administrations and sample groups
- Valid – measures of what the tests set out to measure

The individual benefits from equality and fairness of treatment for all test takers. All candidates are being assessed against each other, under controlled conditions, regardless of gender, diversity of background and age.

BENEFITS OF TESTING TO YOUR ORGANISATION

Testing can help you to:

- Identify applicants with the potential to fit job demands and be high performers (recruitment, selection and promotion)
- Aid understanding of individuals and team members and their possible interaction (personal and team development)
- Improve the motivation and morale of those tested, through acknowledgement of their contribution to success (organisational development)
- Increase retention – using your knowledge and understanding of staff's strengths to place them in appropriate functions
- Develop benchmarks – to identify star performers
- Clearly demonstrate fairness and equal opportunities for all
- Demonstrate consistency over time – using reliable and valid methods of assessment
- Reduce time, costs and mismatches in recruitment and selection – adding to the bottom-line
- Assist with group training and individual coaching
- *Read the pulse* before and after major organisational change – eg downsizing, acquisitions and mergers

DEFINITION

Put simply, psychometric means 'mental measurement', so a psychometric test can measure aspects of the individual such as ability, personality, motivation, competencies, behaviours and interests.

The word test is generic: it is applied generally to all instruments. Some 'tests' are not tests *per se*, so we interchangeably use words like questionnaire, inventory, tool, assessment or instrument.

> *'A psychological test is any procedure on the basis of which inferences are made concerning a person's capacity, propensity or liability to act, react, experience, or to structure or order thought or behaviour in particular ways.'*
> **The British Psychological Society**

WHAT MAKES A GOOD PSYCHOMETRIC TEST?
A GOOD TEST HAS MUSCLE & ENDURANCE

There are two main types of psychometric tests used in the workplace:

- Tests of **maximum** performance, ie general ability tests
- Tests of **typical** performance, ie personality or interest inventories

The British Psychological Society has set up a certificate scheme for test users: the Level A and B Certificates of Competence in Occupational Testing. The authors recommend that all test users seek certification in test use in order to maintain professional standards. Details are given at the end of this pocketbook.

A well constructed test goes together with the ingredients of reliability and validity like honey goes with bees. You cannot have one without the other.

SELECTING THE RIGHT TEST

It is no exaggeration to say that the market place is flooded with psychometric tests (10,000 at a low estimate!). Many produce professional looking reports that at first sight can appear impressive. Some of these tests, however, may not carry a robust body of research behind them in order to satisfy high reliability and validity.

Any good test should be fully researched and rigorously tested before being let loose in the marketplace and made available to the largely unsuspecting general public.

Cautionary tale:
An unfortunate HR officer bought an off-the-shelf psychometric test to use when recruiting for a sales position. The test was supposed to identify a positive, self-starting, confident and extravert person. How come they ended up with someone full of doom and gloom?

Answer: although the test stated that it could measure the above positive attributes, it was not valid, failing to measure what it purported to measure, with potentially disastrous consequences.

INGREDIENTS OF A GOOD TEST

To help avoid the pitfalls of selecting an inappropriate psychometric test, here is a checklist of core questions to ask:

✔ Is there a user's guide or technical manual stating what statistical trials the test has been through and explaining how to administer, score, analyse and interpret?

✔ Has the test been trialled on a large (well over 500) representative sample of people?

✔ What is the test's reliability strength? Does it give consistent results, day after day? You can easily check by reading the research and looking at the test review at the British Psychological Society psychometric testing website – **www.psychtesting.org.uk**

✔ Has the test been validated across cultures, occupations, age and gender and norms produced for each group? Any valid test measures what it purports to measure, eg an aspect of self such as ability, personality, behaviour, intelligence, motivation or aptitude

✔ Are faking detectors built in to check for signs of manipulation from the test taker?

When choosing any test, it is essential that it matches a careful job analysis of the attributes actually required to do the job. **Look beyond the glossy cover of any test.**

GOOD PRACTICE

Test takers have a right to know:

- How their results will be used and interpreted
- Whether the test users are competent to score and interpret results
- How test scores will be communicated and to whom
- Who will have access to results
- How confidentiality will be protected
- How long test scores will be stored
- What assurances will be given to ensure that test scores are not used for purposes other than those agreed with the test taker
- What feedback will be given
- That the tests are properly constructed

Test takers should be given a contact name or phone number if there are any questions or issues to be raised. In team settings, team members should agree how their results should be shared amongst each other with respect only to making the team more efficient.

INTRODUCTION

GOOD PRACTICE

Tests should never be used as a sole means of making personnel decisions because:

- A single measure of a person only looks at that person in one way, from one perspective. This may not be enough in the complex nature of work today. Ability or personality is not everything at work; motivation, interests, sociability, emotional intelligence, track record, experience are all important and need to be taken into account

- All tests are subject to error, and can never be 100% accurate. Error occurs in the way that candidates interpret the words in the questions, error exists in the person, error will occur in the test administration and differences in scores have been noticed according to the time of day of testing. One reason untrained people should not use psychological tests is that they may not understand 'error of measurement' and place too much emphasis on accuracy of test results

After all, a tailor or dressmaker needs considerably more than one set of measurements to make a well-fitting garment.

TESTING FOR SELECTION

WHY USE SELECTION TESTS?

The rationale behind using tests in selection is the better an individual performs on a test, the better that individual will perform in the workplace.

In this chapter we will look at a few scenarios in which selection tests can be used effectively when recruiting or selecting people for a job. It needs to be very clear that the skills tested must be specifically applicable in the job. For instance, when selecting a PA it would not be appropriate to test for mechanical or spatial ability.

Tests should not be used on their own, as a sole basis for hiring people, and should never ever be used for the purpose of firing people!

INTELLIGENCE TESTS

Intelligence testing, as a concept, is not generally used in business, but we feel it is useful to discuss it briefly as it forms the basis of ability testing in general.

The concept of the Intelligence Quotient (IQ) was fashionable about fifty years ago and used, for instance, in selecting children at 11+ to enter grammar school. The national average IQ score is 100, so a child who gained a score of 120 would be 20 points above average, and would normally have expected to secure a place at the grammar school.

Testing for **intelligence** in occupational applications like selection is not that useful because of the alarming fact that intelligence peaks at around 17 years of age.

Testing for **ability** is the next best alternative and it is generally recognised that if you have only a short time to assess an applicant for a job, the best way to use that time is to give the applicant an ability test.

USING ABILITY TESTS FOR SELECTION

It can often be very difficult to identify the range of abilities a person possesses when they apply for a job. It can be harder still if they have no formal qualifications, or are applying for a first job or a supervisory or management position for the first time. Ability, in this context, is a level of mental power: the capacity to do something like reading or mental arithmetic.

Ability tests measure an individual's special abilities; for example how well a candidate works with words or numbers. If someone applies for a job in a bank working with figures, a test of numerical ability would highlight their suitability for the job. Or, when recruiting for a trainee airline pilot, it would be important to test applicants for their spatial awareness ability, so that they can land on the correct runway (!), and to look at their logical reasoning, problem solving and stress management abilities.

We are going to highlight a few of these areas by providing case studies of how tests can be used practically within an organisational setting.

THE GOLDEN TRIANGLE

The Golden Triangle in testing for selection:

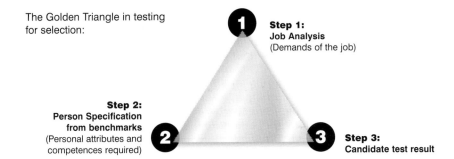

Step 1:
Job Analysis
(Demands of the job)

Step 2:
Person Specification
from benchmarks
(Personal attributes and
competences required)

Step 3:
Candidate test result

In choosing which tests to use, you want to select those that come closest to matching the competences required by the Job Analysis and Person Specification, and matching the person into the job framework.

TESTING FOR SELECTION

GENERAL ABILITY TESTS (GAT 2)

CASE STUDY

A nationwide bakery had for many years been using the **General Ability Tests** (GAT 2 Verbal and Numerical) as part of their recruitment process. After conducting an internal review of the company's use of psychometrics for selection and development, a decision was made to undertake a study involving the bakery's 45 area and production managers. The purpose was to collect a batch of in-house 'norms' and to look at how the tests predicted workplace performance. Norms are established by obtaining a representative sample of successful job holders' scores on GAT2. These scores are then used as a benchmark for the comparison of future job applicants' test scores against those of successful incumbent individuals.

To assure existing employees of the confidentiality of the testing process, an external organisation was called in to process the test results and undertake the data analysis.

There are five GAT2 tests which make up the battery of tests for ability. The tests give a clear indication of an individual's general intellectual ability regardless of education or previous experience.

Used with the kind permission of ASE.

GENERAL ABILITY TESTS (GAT 2)

CASE STUDY

The five GAT2 tests are:

1. **Verbal** – Measures the ability to reason with words through the use of analogies (used in this study to gather internal norms).

2. **Non-Verbal** – Measures the ability to process information, recognise relationships and differentiate between relevant and irrelevant information.

3. **Numerical** – Measures the ability to identify relationships between numbers but without the need for extensive mathematical knowledge (used in this study to gather internal norms).

4. **Spatial** – Measures the ability to visualise objects in 3D (ideal when assessing for positions which involve the manipulation of 3D objects).

5. **Mechanical** – Measures the ability to visualise relationships between moving parts and the way in which mechanical systems operate.

The tests can be administered individually, or in any combination, as in this case.

Used with the kind permission of ASE.

GENERAL ABILITY TESTS (GAT 2)

CASE STUDY: CONCLUSION

The assessments are presented in a 'text free' format. The scores are not influenced by reading comprehension and are therefore fairer to individuals from different cultures or educational backgrounds.

The outcome of the study showed there to be a significant relationship between performance on both the Verbal and Numerical tests and performance on the job. The bakery is now continuing to collect relevant on-going test data to add to their internal norms. Furthermore, they have now fully integrated the GAT2 test battery into their recruitment processes. Both recruitment and retention in the company have been improved by using these norms as benchmarks.

Next we will look at aptitude tests.

Used with the kind permission of ASE.

APTITUDE TESTS

An aptitude is a natural ability to be good at something, eg hand-eye co-ordination for juggling, or ball skills for tennis. An aptitude test predicts how good someone is likely to be at acquiring a new skill or body of knowledge, determining a person's ability in that skill *(Cook & Cripps, 2005)* such as learning a new computer skill.

Sometimes aptitude tests can be combined to form a multiple aptitude battery such as the Computer Programmers Aptitude Battery, which is ideal for assessing computer programmers and systems analysts. This test will be highlighted in the following case study.

You may notice that the use of the words **ability** and **aptitude** by test publishers is very finely drawn and may overlap. This fine distinction takes nothing away from the actual tests.

TESTING FOR SELECTION

APTITUDE TESTS

CASE STUDY: CPAB

An aerospace company was looking internally to promote a project manager from five existing systems analysts. Amongst the measures used for assessment was the **Computer Programmers Aptitude Battery (CPAB)**. They decided to use this measure as a screen to identify a final shortlist of two candidates for further assessment.

The CPAB is ideal for recruiting computer programmers or systems analysts, for assessing both the development needs of existing staff and potential trainees. It consists of five modular timed tests, measuring the following skills and aptitudes:

1. **Verbal Meaning (8 mins)**: tests communication skills and knowledge of vocabulary commonly used in mathematical, business and systems engineering literature.
2. **Reasoning (20 mins)**: tests ability to translate ideas and operations from word problems into mathematical notations.
3. **Letter Series (10 mins)**: tests abstract reasoning ability, finding a pattern in the given series of letters.
4. **Number Ability (6 mins)**: tests ability to quickly estimate reasonable answers to computations.
5. **Diagramming (5 mins)**: tests ability to analyse a problem and order the steps for solution in a logical sequence.

Used with the kind permission of ASE.

APTITUDE TESTS

SCORING SYSTEMS

All psychometric tests use scoring systems so that candidates can be compared with each other. The most common scoring systems are set out below.

Each item that candidates score correctly earns them one point; this is called their raw score. Using tables, these raw scores are converted into:

- **T-score** (transformed score, on a scale of 20-80)
- **Percentile** (score level below which others may have scored)
- **Sten** (score out of 10)
- **Grade** (A-E)

APTITUDE TESTS

CASE STUDY: CPAB RESULTS

The line manager and HR director were presented with the following data:

Name	Verbal Meaning		Reasoning		Letter Series		Number Ability		Diagramming		Decision
	Sten	%ile	Sten	%ile	Sten	%ile	Sten	%ile	Sten	%ile	
AB	5	42	6	58	5	42	4	22	3	12	Not progressed
CD	9	96	8	92	9	96	7	78	9	96	Shortlisted
EF	6	58	7	78	6	58	5	42	7	78	Not progressed*
GH	3	12	4	22	5	42	3	12	4	22	Not progressed
IJ	7	78	7	78	8	92	8	92	8	92	Shortlisted

*Not progressed (but keep on file with consent)

- Candidate **CD: Sten results are 9, 8, 9, 7, 9 at 96th percentile**
- Candidate IJ : **Sten results are 7, 7, 8, 8, 8, at 92nd percentile**

The candidates also took further assessments, including work performance measures and management reports. After consideration of all the results it was decided that **AB** and **GH** would not progress further on this occasion. **EF** scored just above average and, although not moved on to the management stream, will be considered for future supervisor training.

Used with the kind permission of ASE.

CRITICAL REASONING TESTS

We look next at critical reasoning tests.

In today's very fast moving business environment sometimes more general, rather than specific, abilities are required of managers. This is particularly so in the financial sector of a business. Financial directors need not only to understand the precise detail of financial management but also require a broader, more general understanding of the wider business context so that they can match their financial strategies against those of their competitors.

Tests have been designed to look broadly at the wider competence of **critically analysing** situations and data.

The following case study demonstrates how a critical reasoning test can be beneficial in an organisational setting.

CRITICAL REASONING TESTS

CASE STUDY: W-GCTA^{UK}

The board of a publishing house marketing a fashion, food and lifestyle weekly are seeking to recruit a new finance director. They are keen to appoint someone with more than just sound financial competence. The fast-moving, dynamic fashion environment demands someone responsive to change and innovation, with a broad understanding of the publishing world but, above all, with the ability critically to appraise the marketplace and competitors' tactics and strategy.

The CEO has employed a headhunter for the search and has heard that the **Watson Glaser Critical Thinking Appraisal (WGCTA)** can identify competencies relevant to the post, including the ability to think critically and appraise business situations rapidly, considered essential for this position.

The W-GCTA was developed by Goodwin Watson (1925) and Edward Glaser (1937), with the intention of combining theoretical aspects of critical thinking with the practical issues of producing measures that could be used in organisational settings. Professor John Rust (2002) has produced the latest UK version referred to as the **W-GCTA^{UK}**.

CRITICAL REASONING TESTS

HOW THE W-GCTA^{UK} TEST WORKS

The **W-GCTA^{UK}** includes problems, statements, arguments and interpretations: processes similar to those encountered on a daily basis in various responsible management roles.

The W-GCTA^{UK} measures five areas of critical thinking capability, based on an individual's ability to:

1. Make accurate inferences.
2. Recognise assumptions.
3. Evaluate argument.
4. Deduce reasoning.
5. Interpret information logically.

TESTING FOR SELECTION

CRITICAL REASONING TESTS

CASE STUDY: W-GCTA^{UK}

The headhunter agrees that the W-GCTA^{UK} is an appropriate test for the finance director post in this organisation and sets up a testing session for a shortlist of five candidates.

The Watson-Glaser is an easy-to-administer measure of analytical reasoning skills. Each candidate's task is to read a passage from the question booklet, consider a series of propositions relating to given statements, study each statement and evaluate how appropriate or valid these propositions are.

The CEO has asked the headhunter to supply her with a list of the top three candidates' scores, together with a range of assessment centre exercises including scores from The Rust Advanced Numerical Reasoning Appraisal (RANRA), used to assess numerical critical thinking skills relevant to financial competence.

The results table for W-GCTA^{UK} is shown on the next page.

CRITICAL REASONING TESTS

CASE STUDY: W-GCTA^{UK} TABLE OF RESULTS

Name	Inference-raw score out of 16	Recognition of assumptions	Deduction	Interpretation	Evaluation of arguments	Total raw score	T-Score	Percentile	Sten	Grade	Decision
AB	10	12	13	15	15	65	59	82	7	B	2nd interview
CD	8	10	11	10	12	51	43	24	4	C	Not called for interview
EF	13	13	13	13	13	65	59	82	7	B	2nd interview

CRITICAL REASONING TESTS

CASE STUDY: W-GCTA^{UK} CONCLUSION

Looking at each candidate's scores, the CEO observes that **AB** and **EF** have the same **raw score of 65** (actual scores on the test), but the distribution of those scores between tests and between candidates is very different. It looks as if **EF** is more consistent, scoring **13** for each element. The CEO considers this consistency to be a valuable attribute and will invite **AB** and **EF** back for a second interview, after the results of further exercises undertaken in the assessment centre have been analysed.

CD's application will not be taken further.

It is important at this point to remind ourselves that personnel decisions **should not be taken on tests results alone**. This is why the CEO is asking for results from other exercises to be considered.

PERSONALITY TESTS

THE MYTH OF THE PERFECT PERSONALITY

Having looked at aptitude and critical reasoning tests, we now move on to personality tests.

It is important to state that there is no such thing as a perfect personality for any work situation or other context in testing. The 'perfect personality profile' approach (where people believe that there is an ideal profile to fit a job) is a fallacious argument containing several pitfalls:

- Most perfect profiles are derived from people doing the job, taking no account of how **well** they do it

- A perfect profile may show how well people have adapted to the job's demands, not how well people with that profile are naturally comfortable with doing the job

- The perfect profile approach encourages cloning – only selecting as managers people who closely resemble existing managers. This may create great harmony and satisfaction within the organisation, but could make the organisation very vulnerable and too comfortable when faced with the need to change. Diversity of personality is often an advantage, in any organisation

PERSONALITY TESTS

There are hundreds of personality tests available and it is very difficult even for the expert to choose the test that fits all situations; it is a bit like choosing a single pair of shoes to suit all the activities you might do on holiday: walking, playing sport, dancing or going to a smart restaurant.

Instead, when thinking of applying a personality test, we should perhaps ask how a person with a particular personality profile or personality traits is likely to perform in the context we are considering, which is – how the organisation can best meet its development objectives through the greater understanding of an individual's personality.

On the next few pages we illustrate, through a case study in development, a foundation test: the **16 Personality Factor Questionnaire** (16PF®5). Dr Raymond Cattell wrote the 16PF as part of his work to identify the primary components of personality. His research was based on the use of factor analysis to interpret data derived from questionnaire items and from behavioural ratings. This test has an extensive pedigree of research reliability and validity, gathered over the last 60 years, and is of particular use in selection, personal development and change.

PERSONALITY TESTS

CASE STUDY: 16PF PROFILE

A large retailer looking to fill the position of call centre manager by an internal promotion was advised to use the 16PF (5th Edition). Zofia, one of those being considered, came across at work as confident and keen to take on more responsibility.

These traits were supported by her profile (see page 36) which shows a just above average level of confidence (sten 7-socially bold, Factor H) and a preference for taking the lead and being in control (sten 8-dominance, Factor E). The profile also shows less suitable traits. A sten 2 score for emotional stability (Factor C) suggests someone reactive, prone to mood swings and not calm under pressure. This could affect her management of customers and staff, particularly with a low score for warmth (sten 1-warmth, Factor A) and high physical tension (sten 9-tension, Factor Q4) indicating an amount of restless impatience.

Her enthusiastic approach to work is shown by a sten 8 score for liveliness (Factor F) but a high score for vigilance (sten 10-vigilance, Factor L) suggests she may be suspicious of other people's views and motives, leading her to reject their opinions and ideas in an inflexible way. Her tolerance for disorder and leaving things to chance (sten 3-perfectionism, Factor Q3) may impede her ability to drive for results and motivate others.

PERSONALITY TESTS

CASE STUDY: 16PF PROFILE

		Sten		1	2	3	4	5	6	7	8	9	10	
Warmth	(A)	1	Reserved	●										Warm
Reasoning	(B)	7	Concrete							●				Abstract
Emotional stability	(C)	2	Reactive		●									Emotionally stable
Dominance	(E)	8	Deferential								●			Dominant
Liveliness	(F)	8	Serious								●			Lively
Rule-consciousness	(G)	2	Expedient		●									Rule-conscious
Social boldness	(H)	7	Shy							●				Socially bold
Sensitivity	(I)	6	Utilitarian						●					Sensitive
Vigilance	(L)	10	Trusting										○	Vigilant
Abstractedness	(M)	10	Grounded										○	Abstracted
Privateness	(N)	6	Forthright						●					Private
Apprehension	(O)	9	Self-assured									●		Apprehensive
Openness to change	(Q1)	3	Traditional			●								Open to change
Self-reliance	(Q2)	6	Group-oriented						●					Self-reliant
Perfectionism	(Q3)	3	Tolerates disorder			●								Perfectionistic
Tension	(Q4)	9	Relaxed									●		Tense

PERSONALITY TESTS
CASE STUDY: 16PF CONCLUSION

The HR director, in consultation with the managing director, decided not to promote Zofia but, in order to maintain her motivation and utilise her outstanding product knowledge, she was offered external coaching.

This 16PF profile, used in conjunction with discussions with Zofia, and other evidence of how she related to her colleagues, helped Zofia's manager take an appropriate and agreed set of decisions, which worked to Zofia's advantage.

Here then is an example of using a psychometric test which presents a rather negative picture of a person to support other information, like workplace reports and interviews, to make personnel decisions **to the advantage of the organisation and the candidate**.

PERSONALITY TESTS

PERSONALITY OR BEHAVIOUR

Personality traits can be reliably tested by most valid and reliable instruments. Research shows that these traits do not transfer absolutely into behaviour in the workplace. This is because the workplace environment will cause some change of the pure personality trait into the accepted workplace culture of an organisation. Workplace behaviour can be modified by the situation; tests can help indicate possible directions for such modification.

Some instruments, because they are designed to pick up these working style behaviours, are particularly appropriate to use in measuring the way that people may use their personality to form their own particular management style. This will be demonstrated in the next psychometric instrument, the **Personal Profile Analysis**, and accompanying **Human Job Analysis**. These instruments offer useful insights into work style behaviours demanded of a particular job function.

WORK STYLE TESTS

CASE STUDY: THOMAS INTERNATIONAL SYSTEM PPA

An organisation that specialises in selling off-plan properties around the globe, from Spain to the Caribbean, is looking to recruit a sales person to work in their international office in Spain. The ability to speak Spanish will be an important attribute in the selection process in order to understand local property processes adequately and communicate fluently in both English and Spanish.

Three Spanish speakers have been short-listed and asked to complete a work style inventory, following the Thomas International System.

WORK STYLE TESTS

HOW THE THOMAS SYSTEM PPA WORKS

The work style inventory selected was the **Thomas International Personal Profile Analysis (PPA)**. The PPA is designed around the DISC model of workplace behaviour. The history of the DISC models of assessment is grounded in the psychological theory of sensing, intuition, thinking and feeling developed in the 1920s by Carl G Jung in his book *The Psychological Types*. It was in 1928 that William Moulton Marston highlighted in his book, *Emotions of Normal People* the types **D** = Dominance, **I** = Inducement, **S** = Submission and **C** = Compliance (DISC) as types of behavioural response to a perceived friendly or hostile environment.

The types and trait words that have been interpreted by Thomas International are:

		HIGH	LOW
D	Dominance	driving, competitive, direct	modest, peaceful, unassuming
I	Influence	optimistic, self-promoting	reserved, reflective, retiring
S	Steadiness	dependable, self-controlled, easy-going	impatient, mobile, active
C	Compliance	disciplined, perfection-seeking, logical	firm, obstinate, persistent

Some material copyright Thomas International Ltd, reproduced here with their permission.

TESTING FOR SELECTION

WORK STYLE TESTS

CASE STUDY: THOMAS SYSTEM PPA

The Thomas System PPA comprises three main assessments: the Human Job Analysis (HJA), which analyses a job in terms of DISC; the Personal Profile Analysis (PPA), measuring the personal attributes of a candidate; and finally Ability Tests for Selection and Training (which we do not go into here).

The company selected this particular inventory because the combination of Personal Profile Analysis and Human Job Analysis, completed by the organisation and outlining the necessary job requirements involved in selling off-plan properties, is a compact model looking at both job and person in the same terms.

The requirements revealed by the HJA for this position are:

- Strong influencing skills
- Assertiveness
- Fast pace of operation in a dynamic environment

TESTING FOR SELECTION

WORK STYLE TESTS

THOMAS SYSTEM PPA

The Thomas System PPA provides insight into workplace behaviour looking at:

- Strengths and limitations – current job performance in terms of behavioural preferences in a work context

- Ability to self-start – get up and go without prompting

- Communication style – how a manager may interact with others with respect to their preferred behavioural style

- Motivation – motivational patterns as derived from workplace preferences

WORK STYLE TESTS

THOMAS SYSTEM PPA PROCEDURE

The PPA provides a profile measuring the key behavioural characteristics or workplace style of an individual at work. A series of 24 questions on a forced choice, ipsative (self-referential), 'first impressions' basis, outlines candidates' styles on four main dimensions: Dominance, Influence, Steadiness and Compliance (DISC).

When used for selection, the PPA should be preceded by the Human Job Analysis (HJA) which first identifies the behavioural requirements of a job. Like the PPA, the results are plotted on a graph which provides an objective view of a particular role and indicates the behavioural style of the person most likely to succeed. The PPA profile is then compared with the HJA to look at how well the two profiles fit.

WORK STYLE TESTS

CASE STUDY: THOMAS SYSTEM PPA

The time share company asks three people who know the job well to draw up a job analysis in the profile form of the **Human Job Analysis (HJA)**. The results are plotted on a graph, see next page. Then two short-listed candidates are profiled using the **PPA**, see second and third graphs. Finally, the candidates will be interviewed.

In the HJA profile for the job, the work style of the sales person demands a high level (above centre line) of Dominance and Influence and a lower level (below centre line) of Steadiness and Compliance.

The initial interview with each candidate will be structured to confirm (or deny) their PPA findings and then confirm whether or not the candidate at interview behaves according to their profile or modifies their behaviour (impression management) to influence the interviewers, very common in high stakes situations like recruitment.

The profile graph shows that Candidate 1 fits the HJA most closely. This was confirmed by the structured interview, and he will proceed to the next stage. Candidate 2 reports himself as fitting the job in only two of the scales, so may not feel comfortable in the role.

WORK STYLE INVENTORY

CASE STUDY: THOMAS SYSTEM PPA PROFILES

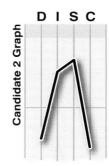

High D & I
Low S & C

High D & I
Low S & C
Fit organisation is looking for

High I & S
Low D & C
Poor fit

WORK STYLE INVENTORY
CASE STUDY: THOMAS SYSTEM PPA CONCLUSION

The Thomas System is designed to fit 'round pegs into round holes'. It helps us understand that if we can outline the behavioural aspects of a job and then fill that position with a candidate whose behavioural style closely matches the requirements of that job then job satisfaction, retention, productivity and the bottom line should all be improved.

46

TESTING FOR ORGANISATIONAL DEVELOPMENT

WHAT IS ORGANISATIONAL DEVELOPMENT?

Organisational development (OD) has been defined as *'the process of planned change, learning and development, and improvement in the organisation through the application of knowledge of behavioural sciences'*. (Moorhead & Griffin, Organisational behaviour: managing people and organisations)

In simple terms, it means that the application of psychometric tests can help to improve the performance of individuals, teams and the organisation as a whole because tests can measure, as part of the process, **the potential for performance**.

In today's changing and volatile world, organisations are continually looking for ways to improve performance and satisfy the demands of their customers, clients and other key stakeholders. For an organisation to evolve, the people working within it will have to adapt; and for this to be successful, they first of all need to know what it is about the way they are currently performing that needs to change.

We next describe a case study using emotional intelligence (EI) in OD.

WHAT IS EMOTIONAL INTELLIGENCE (EI)?

EI is about the ability to understand oneself and express feelings, to understand how others feel and be able to relate to them, and to change and manage emotional behaviours in a positive way.

The words 'emotional intelligence' were first used by B. Leuner in 1966, nearly a quarter of a century before Peter Salovey and John Mayer's first article appeared on the topic in 1990. Salovey and Mayer are both highly regarded psychologists still active in the field of EI. It is, however, Daniel Goleman, author of *'Emotional Intelligence'* (1995), and *'Working with Emotional Intelligence'* (1998) who has played the most critical role in the creation of the opportunities for the EI field.

Goleman writes and talks about emotional intelligence in ways that receive the attention of people outside the field of psychology and he has put EI onto the world map. From being a taboo topic in the business arena, emotions are now mentioned in workplace settings. To quote Daniel Goleman, 'The rules for work are changing and being judged by a new yardstick, not just how smart we are, or our expertise, but also how well we handle ourselves and each other'.

USING EI TESTS FOR ORGANISATIONAL DEVELOPMENT

Organisations facing 21st century challenges of globalisation, downsizing, merging or restructuring, require their people to be more accountable and more visible within the organisation. These new challenges demand new personal qualities such as taking the initiative, empathy, adaptability and teamwork.

The notion that EI matters at work is now very compelling. We all have seen situations in the workplace where emotions and feelings have had a very real impact on the quality of interactions, relationships and behaviours, affecting the performance of the organisation as a whole. A phrase often heard: 'people don't leave jobs, they leave managers' perhaps emphasises the importance of an understanding of EI.

EMOTIONAL INTELLIGENCE

CASE STUDY: BAR-ON EQ-I

A large banking organisation was looking for a team leader to promote within their IT department. The candidate selected for the job seemed an ideal choice. Matteo had left university with a first class degree in Computing, followed by a Masters degree in Systems Analysis. He was, without doubt, very bright and focused on his job and quickly gathered expertise at systems problem solving. Matteo accepted the promotion and became team leader of a group of 10 people. He had never actually managed people before, only a square box in front of him, which did not answer back!

Matteo's lack of people skills soon created tensions within the team. HR, after consultation with his manager, decided to refer him to an executive coach. The coach wanted to help Matteo understand himself better as a way to nurture his people skills and manage more positively his social interactions with his team. It was decided to administer the **Bar-On Emotional Quotient Inventory (EQ-i)**, developed by Dr Reuven Bar-On. The EQ-i is a measure of emotionally and socially intelligent behaviour **which provides an estimate of one's underlying emotional-social intelligence.**

EMOTIONAL INTELLIGENCE

CASE STUDY: BAR-ON EQ-I

Dr Reuven Bar-On began his work in the field of EI in the 1980s. He was perplexed by a number of questions:

- Why do some people possess greater well-being?

- Why are some people better able to achieve success in life?

- Why do some people who may be blessed with superior intelligence abilities seem to do less well in life, while others with lower intelligence succeed? *S. Stein & H Book: 2001, 2006*

Dr Bar-On originally suggested that effective emotional and social functioning has a positive impact on performance at home, school and in the workplace; and he later developed a number of psychometric instruments to examine this idea.

Returning to the case study, Matteo may have been so focused on studying for his exams that the emotional and social functioning side of his personality was under-developed.

On the following page are the 5 composite scales and 15 subscales which the EQ-i measured when Matteo took the test.

TESTING FOR ORGANISATIONAL DEVELOPMENT

EMOTIONAL INTELLIGENCE

BAR-ON EQ-I

The instrument is composed of the five scales below that measure the following EI factors, competencies and skills:

- **Intrapersonal** measures the inner self – emotional self-awareness, independence, assertiveness, self-regard and self-actualisation

- **Interpersonal** measures relationship skills – empathy, interpersonal skills and social responsibility

- **Adaptability** measures how we assess and respond to situations – flexibility, reality testing and problem solving

- **Stress management** measures the ability to handle stressful situations without falling apart – stress tolerance and impulse control

- **General mood** measures our outlook on life – self-motivation, optimism and happiness

Used with the kind permission of MHS Multi-Health Systems Inc.

(53)

EMOTIONAL INTELLIGENCE

CASE STUDY: BAR-ON EQ-I

Matteo completed the EQ-i online using a confidential login and password. The 133 responses to the questionnaire were scored and a fully interpretative user-friendly report was printed in readiness for face-to-face feedback of the results.

Matteo's responses to the questionnaire, examined during the feedback session with his coach, indicated how the various aspects of his emotional intelligence impacted on his behaviour at work. The test results revealed the difficulties he was experiencing when dealing with people and managing stressful situations. His inability to control his temper made his team feel very negative towards him.

TESTING FOR ORGANISATIONAL DEVELOPMENT

EMOTIONAL INTELLIGENCE
CASE STUDY: BAR-ON EQ-I

In discussion with the coach it was decided to work on the following areas of Matteo's emotional intelligence:

- Social awareness and training in interpersonal skills
- Strategies to better manage the emotions of his work colleagues
- Understanding that people as individuals are all different
- Greater flexibility and responsibility in his social interactions
- Improved emotional control to minimise or remove emotional outbursts

As part of the psychometric testing evaluation process, the EQ-i should be administered again after six months to see if there has actually been a change in Matteo's emotional intelligence. A 360 degree feedback assessment is an effective method for understanding workplace performance and will be used for this evaluation.

EMOTIONAL INTELLIGENCE

MULTI-RATER 360 EI FEEDBACK

Multi-rater 360 EI feedback is a process whereby an individual (the recipient) is rated on his or her emotional intelligence by people (the raters) who know the person, their work and behaviour. Raters can include direct reports, peers and managers and, in some cases, customers or clients. In fact, anybody who is credible to the individual and is familiar with their work can be included in the feedback process.

For an organisation to evolve, the people working within it, such as Matteo, need to adapt to the changes going on around them.

For Matteo to succeed in adapting, he needs to know what it is about his management style that needs to change. He has now found this out and a developmental action plan for behaviour change has been drawn up for him. Six months after administering the EQ-i is an appropriate time to re-evaluate, to see if a change has actually taken place in his emotional intelligence.

The aim of the resulting information is to indicate to the recipient how he is perceived by others.

Used with the kind permission of MHS Multi-Health Systems Inc.

TESTING FOR ORGANISATIONAL DEVELOPMENT

EMOTIONAL INTELLIGENCE

EQ-360

The EQ-360, a multi-rater tool designed to assess emotional intelligence, was developed by Reuven Bar-On and Richard Handley. It was selected to evaluate Matteo because it fully complements the EQ-i measure of social and emotional intelligence, in that the questions Matteo had been asked when he originally completed the EQ-i were now being asked of his peers, managers, direct reports and other appropriate raters.

In order to identify any specific changes in emotionally and socially intelligent behaviour, and to see if there is congruency between Matteo and his raters, he completes the EQ-i again. All responses are confidential and it is important to make sure that there is a fair share of raters for each category of peers, managers and direct reports.

Matteo's EQ-i scores were noticeably congruent with his raters' scoring in the areas of enhanced interpersonal skills and impulse control. With training, Matteo had been made aware of how emotional and social intelligence could help him manage and lead his team more effectively.

EMOTIONAL INTELLIGENCE

EQ-360

OTHER BENEFITS TO THE ORGANISATION

Professionally managed, EQ 360 feedback increases individual self-awareness, and as part of a strategic organisational process can promote:

- Increased understanding of the behaviours required to improve both individual and organisational effectiveness

- More focused development activities, built around the skills and competencies required for successful organisational performance

- Increased involvement of people at all levels of the organisation

- Increased individual ownership for self-development and learning

- Increased familiarity with the implications of robust feedback on self-performance in the workplace

"O wad some power the giftie gie us

To see oursels as ithers see us!"

From To a Louse by Robert Burns

TESTING FOR ORGANISATIONAL DEVELOPMENT

WELL-BEING & QUALITY OF WORKING LIFE

We are now going to review an OD test which looks at an employee's quality of life.

While financial rewards remain an important source of motivation to some employees, this form of external motivation alone is not enough. Employees have higher expectations of what they want from their employment and are increasingly likely to change companies (and even countries) in search of job satisfaction as part of that elusive quality of life.

In excess of half a million people in the UK at any one time experience stress at levels that make them ill.

Organisations now need to show they are seriously commited to the welfare of their employees, by providing good working conditions leading to a high quality of working life. Our case study illustrates a test that not only helps organisations to attract staff, but also helps to retain existing staff by measuring perceptions on the quality of life in that organisation.

TESTING FOR ORGANISATIONAL DEVELOPMENT

WELL-BEING

CASE STUDY: QUALITY OF WORKING LIFE QUESTIONNAIRE

The HR manager for a city company raised concern about employee welfare. A yearly staff attendance check had highlighted a higher than expected level of time off work. Analysis of the reasons given revealed high levels of stress, anxiety and other illness, with comments made about the quality of working life in the organisation.

An urgent meeting was held, and the decision taken to undertake an organisational audit to assess the health and well-being climate. The questionnaire selected was the **Quality of Working Life Questionnaire**. It can be used in the following ways at the following levels:

- Across an organisation
- With smaller groups of employees
- When working with individuals

TESTING FOR ORGANISATIONAL DEVELOPMENT

WELL-BEING

QUALITY OF WORKING LIFE QUESTIONNAIRE

Unlike the other tests mentioned throughout this pocketbook, no formal training is required to use this questionnaire.

The questionnaire measures seven aspects of working life:

1. Support from a manager or supervisor.
2. Freedom from work-related stress.
3. Salary and additional benefits.
4. Job satisfaction, challenge, use of skill and autonomy.
5. Relationships with work colleagues.
6. Involvement and responsibility at work.
7. Communication, decision making and job security.

Used with the kind permission of ASE.

TESTING FOR ORGANISATIONAL DEVELOPMENT

WELL-BEING

CASE STUDY: QUALITY OF WORKING LIFE QUESTIONNAIRE

Individuals rated their responses on a five point scale: from strongly agree to strongly disagree. The results were then processed by a software program and reports generated that gave the HR manager a good overview of the perceived quality of working life.

The results showed that there was indeed a higher than normal level of dissatisfaction across the seven aspects measured. The company decided to introduce a well-being programme including in-house relaxation therapists, a gym facility and employee assistance programmes. It was also decided that after six months the quality of life questionnaire would be run again to compare any changes in the perceived quality of working life across the organisation.

"Just off to the well-being centre for a massage, boss....."

TESTING FOR ORGANISATIONAL DEVELOPMENT

MANAGEMENT DEVELOPMENT

A series of questionnaires designed to measure management style, motivation, talent and preferred culture, known as **Saville Consulting Wave**® was launched by Saville Consulting in 2005. The Professional Styles Expert Report, developed by Professor Peter Saville (MacIver et. al., 2006) measures participants in three ways:

1. Exploration of **motives, preferences, needs and talents** in critical work clusters, eg:
    - **Thought** – vision, judgement and evaluation
    - **Influence** – leadership, impact and communication
    - **Adaptability** – support, resilience and flexibility
    - **Delivery** – structure, drive and implementation

2. A measure of Predicted Culture/Environment Fit, indicating those aspects of the culture of the organisation, job and environment likely to enhance or inhibit a person's success.

3. The Competency Potential Report, linking the questionnaire responses to real data on work performance validated on over 1,000 professionals giving a unique prediction of candidates' likely strengths and limitations in 36 key performance/competency areas.

Used with the kind permission of Saville Consulting Group Ltd. (See page 126 for full reference)

TESTING FOR ORGANISATIONAL DEVELOPMENT

MANAGEMENT DEVELOPMENT

CASE STUDY: SAVILLE CONSULTING WAVE

Simon was being considered for a management role in his engineering company. The People Development director asked him to complete **Wave Professional Styles**. They then reviewed his Competency Potential Profile together. Under the Influence cluster, Simon scored highly on Providing Leadership (Making Decisions, Directing People, Empowering Individuals) indicating suitability for management. Scores for Building Relationships (Interacting with People, Establishing Rapport, Impressing People) were, however, all low.

Simon acknowledged that these areas would need greater focus in a future management position. It was agreed to look at how to develop his skills through a combination of coaching and external training. His readiness for promotion would then be reviewed six months later, when he was more likely to be ready for the new people responsibilities.

Other applications for Wave in the workplace are in **selection**: compatibility and fit, planning, induction, improving motivation, job satisfaction and retention; **development**: aligning motives and talents, building successful teams and improving commitment, and **change**: aligning people to culture change, identifying barriers to change and closing the gap between preferred and actual culture.

TESTING FOR TEAMS

WHY USE TEAM TESTS?

INNOVATION & TEAMWORKING

Teams are increasingly seen as one of the best ways to achieve innovation and improvement in business life. But just calling a diverse group of people a team doesn't always lead to good teamwork. Furthermore, with the challenges of globalisation and rapid change, the single element in the workplace that is likely to remain constant is the need for people to be able to function in work-based groups or teams.

Team tests can be very useful in the following areas:

- Developing stronger, more unified teams who all share the same vision
- Identifying team strengths and weaknesses
- Identifying each team member's role within the team
- Providing role clarity about what is expected from each team member
- Empowering the team's self-awareness through knowing their own individual strengths and limitations, and becoming comfortable with each other
- Strengthening the teams that move the organisation forward, particularly Senior Management Teams
- Identifying teams that integrate well within the wider organisation
- Valuing the diversity of group members and what they have to offer

WHY USE TEAM TESTS?

A team role is defined by Dr Meredith Belbin as: *'a tendency to behave, contribute and interrelate with others in a particular way'*.

In a well run hotel the owner ensures that she employs staff to handle reception, cooking, cleaning and waiting, ie different people to fit different roles to ensure the comfort of the customers. The principles of teamworking rely on having a balanced team of people **fulfilling different functions**, in the same way that they bring their different behaviours to work.

Research has also shown that different combinations of behaviours can create more effective team members. For example, if everyone on the team is bursting with creative ideas but no one likes routine and detail, then the team is likely to be heading for failure. It is, therefore, very important **to have a balanced team taking up different roles** to enhance team performance.

The next case study will demonstrate the significance of having different team roles.

TEAM ROLES

CASE STUDY: BELBIN TEAM ROLES INVENTORY

The owner of a hotel feels that she and her staff of eight people would benefit from a better understanding of their identity as a team. The purpose would be to help the individuals understand:

- Where their strengths lie
- What role they contribute to the team as a whole
- The roles that others play

It will help the team to work more smoothly if each team member understands the roles of others and where they all complement each other.

A business psychologist was called in and the whole team was asked to complete the **Belbin Team Roles Inventory**.

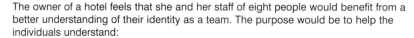

TEAM ROLES

Dr Meredith Belbin and his team of researchers studied the behaviour of managers from all over the world. They wanted to answer the question: why do some teams perform better than others?

The research highlighted the fact that people in teams tend to assume different 'team roles' and the role that each individual plays within the team underlies the team success. Therefore each team member has a vital contribution to make.

The nine team roles, including the latest addition of 'Specialist', are presented on the following pages, which show how each role contributes to the team and what their allowable weaknesses might be.

THE 9 BELBIN TEAM ROLES

SUMMARY DESCRIPTIONS

1. PLANT

Contribution to the team: Creative, imaginative, unorthodox, able to solve difficult problems.

Allowable weakness: Can ignore incidentals, and may be too preoccupied to communicate effectively.

2. RESOURCE INVESTIGATOR

Contribution to the team: Extrovert, enthusiastic, communicative, explores opportunities, develops contacts.

Allowable weakness: Over-optimistic, loses interest once initial enthusiasm has passed.

THE 9 BELBIN TEAM ROLES

SUMMARY DESCRIPTIONS

3. CO-ORDINATOR

Contribution to the team: Mature, confident, a good chairperson, clarifies goals, promotes decision-making, delegates well.

Allowable weakness: Can be seen as manipulative, offloads personal work.

4. SHAPER

Contribution to the team: Challenging, dynamic, thrives on pressure, the drive and courage to overcome obstacles.

Allowable weakness: Prone to provocation, offends people's feelings.

THE 9 BELBIN TEAM ROLES

SUMMARY DESCRIPTIONS

5. MONITOR EVALUATOR

Contribution to the team: Sober, strategic and discerning, sees all options, judges accurately.

Allowable weakness: Lacks drive and ability to inspire others.

6. TEAMWORKER

Contribution to the team: Co-operative, mild, perceptive and diplomatic, listens, builds, averts friction.

Allowable weakness: Indecisive in crunch situations.

THE 9 BELBIN TEAM ROLES

SUMMARY DESCRIPTIONS

7. IMPLEMENTER

Contribution to the team: Disciplined, reliable, conservative and efficient, turns ideas into practical actions.

Allowable weakness: Somewhat inflexible, slow to respond to new possibilities.

8. COMPLETER FINISHER

Contribution to the team: Painstaking, conscientious, anxious, searches out errors and omissions, delivers on time.

Allowable weakness: Inclined to worry unduly, reluctant to delegate.

THE 9 BELBIN TEAM ROLES

SUMMARY DESCRIPTIONS

9. SPECIALIST

Contribution to the team: Single-minded, self-starting, dedicated, provides knowledge and skills in rare supply.

Allowable weakness: Contributes on only a narrow front, dwells on technicalities.

TEAM ROLES

CASE STUDY: BELBIN TEAM ROLES INVENTORY RESULTS

In the hotel, the Belbin results showed the following job functions matching the corresponding roles:

- Owner (1) – Shaper
- Manager (1) – Co-ordinator
- Receptionists (x 2) – Resource Investigator & Teamworker
- Chef (1) – Specialist
- Head Waiter (1) – Completer Finisher
- Waiter (1) – Teamworker
- Kitchen Staff (x 2) – Teamworkers

The team has the right mix of personnel. The owner (Shaper) provides the necessary drive and energy and works well with the manager (Co-ordinator) who can understand the owner's needs and delegate accordingly. The hospitality industry needs plenty of teamworkers, which this team has, to ensure good customer service.

The team lacks an Implementer which might mean poor organisation and use of time. The hotel does achieve results, however. Since individuals rarely have just one preferred behaviour, it could be that the Implementer role features highly on a number of people's profiles. The lack of a Plant in the team is not necessarily a bad thing in this environment, where new ideas and creative solutions to difficult business problems are not really required. (75)

TEAM BUILDING

CASE STUDY: MYERS-BRIGGS TYPE INDICATOR®

The next popular team test we will be looking at is often adopted for team building purposes as well as for personal and organisational development.

A large international construction company has extended its operations to Dubai, and wants a team of people based there to oversee building standards. The HR department decided to run a team building workshop for the five members of the new team, who would be relocating to Dubai from the UK, US and Canada. For the workshop, they chose the world renowned team building tool, **Myers-Briggs Type Indicator® (MBTI®)**.

The MBTI® tool is a personality test designed to assist an individual in identifying some significant preferences. Katharine Briggs and her daughter Isabel Briggs developed the indicator during the Second World War and its scales follow from Carl Jung's themes in his work *Psychological Types*.

The questionnaire is un-timed, self report and asks respondents to choose between two opposing courses of action, or two words, depending on what they feel is closest to their natural preference. These preferences are presented next.

WHAT THE MBTI® TOOL MEASURES

Extraversion (E) – Prefers to draw their energy from the outside world of activity, people and things.

Or

Introversion (I) – Prefers to draw their energy from the inner world of reflections, thoughts, feelings and ideas.

Sensing (S) – Prefers to focus on the present and on concrete information gained from their five senses for perceiving the world around them.

Or

Intuition (N) – Prefers to focus on the future and uses their intuitive side or 'sixth sense' to focus on relationships and possibilities.

WHAT THE MBTI® TOOL MEASURES

Thinking (T) – Prefers to base their decisions on logic and objective analysis of cause and effect.

Or

Feeling (F) – Prefers to base decisions on a valuing process, considering what is important to people.

Judging (J) – Prefers a planned, organised approach to life with quick closure.

Or

Perceiving (P) – Prefers a flexible, spontaneous approach and to keep their options open.

TEAM BUILDING

CASE STUDY MYERS-BRIGGS TYPE INDICATOR® RESULTS

Prior to the workshop, the five participants undertook the tests electronically (using confidential login and passwords). The results (see next page) indicated a substantial amount of similarity among the five members of the new team.

The performance of **highly similar** teams can vary, with some performing quite well and others struggling. Whether a team with a high similarity is successful or not depends on two things:

1. How well the team type fits with the approach required by their task or project.
2. How aware the team is of its blind spots, ie the preferences not covered by anyone on the team.

The results show a team type of ESTJ, although only two of the five have this full profile. (The team type is derived by counting the number of team members with each preference.) What is important here is that the sum of the individual MBTI® profiles forms an overall team style and the task will be completed within that team style of ESTJ, which will be different from some of the team members' preferences.

TEAM BUILDING

CASE STUDY MYERS-BRIGGS TYPE INDICATOR® RESULTS

ISTJ ①	ISFT	INFJ	**INTJ** ①	Extraversion	3	
ISTP	ISFP	INFP	INTP	Introversion	2	*Resulting in a pooled set of preferences of*
				Sensing	4	
ESTP	ESFP	ENFP	ENTP	Intuition	1	
				Thinking	4	***ESTJ***
ESTJ ②	**ESFJ** ①	ENFJ	ENTJ	Feeling	1	
				Judging	5	
				Perceiving	0	

The team has no cover of the **Perceiving** preference, suggesting they may have a lack of flexibility and spontaneity; there may only be limited cover of **Intuition** (future focus and possibilities) and **Feeling** (basing decisions on values and subjective evaluation).

These points will be raised by the facilitator in the team briefing session in order to look at ways forward for the team to help in the overall success of the business.

TESTING FOR TEAMS

HIGH SIMILARITY TEAMS

High similarity amongst team members is normally associated with:

- Finishing tasks more quickly

- Failing to make good use of the resources of the team; perhaps not identifying or using the talents of the right person for the task

- Producing more traditional, less original, solutions to problems

- Producing more limited or constrained solutions than do highly dissimilar teams, as judged by external criteria

- Pressure within the team to solve problems by consensus, which may inhibit the expression of unique individual solution

On the following pages are lists of possible strengths and limitations for an ESTJ team and a contrasting INFP team.

CONTRASTING TEAMS

ESTJ

Possible strengths:

- Decisive and outspoken
- Bases decisions on known facts
- Structured and organised
- Has clear performance expectations
- Achieves practical results
- Keeps bottom line in sight

Possible limitations:

- May reject new ideas
- May be unaware of new trends
- May override important long-range factors for short-term goals (often financial)
- May make decisions without all the information
- May not consider how decisions will affect key stakeholders

CONTRASTING TEAMS

INFP

Possible strengths:

- Creative
- Adaptable
- Counselling approach
- Gently persuasive
- Sense of purpose

Possible limitations:

- May get overwhelmed by possibilities
- May overlook important facts
- May not consider logical consequences of each alternative
- May be overly influenced by what others in the team want
- May be put off making decisions

CONCLUSION

The Belbin instrument and the MBTI® instrument look at teams in different ways. Belbin looks at individual job roles first and the type of tasks that are naturally preferred; the MBTI® tool looks more at personality as a whole and the way that team members' personality preferences group together to make up a team, following the preferred style of the aggregate of those preferences.

As mentioned earlier, a team operates most effectively when a balanced spread of preferences is demonstrated. Do not assume that everyone should have the same type preference.

A team review session should point out possible strengths and limitations while making it clear that type differences are very important. It is particularly important that areas affecting work tasks that are not, or are insufficiently, covered, eg Plant and Implementer in our Belbin example, and INFP preferences in our MBTI® example, should be discussed with team members and management.

Finally, possible blind spots and conflict areas should be confronted and dealt with through discussion with other individuals with different type preferences.

TESTING FOR PERSONAL DEVELOPMENT

TESTING FOR PERSONAL DEVELOPMENT

AT THE CROSSROADS

It is perfectly normal for all of us to want to take a pause in life, reflect on where we are going, to re-appraise our lives, and make decisions about the future before moving on. Occasionally life events may force us to do this, but it is quite natural to want to change just for a change!

At these times we need to address three main questions:

- Where are we now?
- Where do we want to go?
- How do we get there?

WHY PSYCHOMETRIC TESTING?

At these important, life-changing, 'crossroad' times psychometric testing can provide useful signposts. Psychologists tell us that most behaviour is not accidental; it is caused and put into action by our motivation and feelings of satisfying needs, eg:

- Drink when thirsty
- Eat when hungry
- Sleep when tired
- Laugh when happy

A very useful starting point is to use psychometric testing to examine two aspects of our temperament: motivation and personality. Fortunately psychometric test publishers have provided some excellent, valid and reliable instruments to measure these two attributes. We will start by looking at **motivation and a motivational inventory**.

TESTING FOR PERSONAL DEVELOPMENT

MOTIVATION TESTS

Motivation is included here under individual development because in many respects motivation guides our activities throughout the working week, from waking up in the morning to going to bed at night.

When a person is more motivated they:

- Work more productively
- Contribute more to the organisation
- Are more likely to achieve their full potential
- Will gain greater satisfaction from their job
- Have an enhanced feeling of well-being

Unlocking the key to motivation can be a difficult process because all individuals are motivated by different things.

MOTIVATION TESTS

Abraham Maslow's Hierarchy of Needs theory was one of the first motivation theories to be applied to individuals at work. Maslow said that people's wants and needs guide behaviour. According to Maslow, a need influences a person's activities at that level until it has been satisfied, and then the superordinate level need is sought. His theory places five needs in an ascending hierarchy, making the assumption that basic needs are met first. This applies to having food and water, a roof over your head, friends, confidence and a need to self-actualise, a posh word for achieving your life dreams! It is at this self-actualisation point that you are supposed to have reached your full potential as an individual.

Self-actualisation

Self-esteem

Social needs

Security

Basic needs

It is important to understand what motivates people at work in order to understand how to unlock their full potential, increase productivity and enable them to reach that summit.

TESTING FOR PERSONAL DEVELOPMENT

MOTIVATION QUESTIONNAIRE

CASE STUDY: SHL MOTIVATION QUESTIONNAIRE (MQ)

Kerri has just joined a large high street bank arranging mortgages. She was snapped up by the bank because she is very numerate and alert with a bubbly personality. A few weeks into her job, however, the manager has started to receive reports that Kerri is upsetting other members of staff. She complains constantly about the boredom of her job which involves arranging mortgages day after day, week after week, in an ongoing and somewhat mundane routine. Her boss asks the HR department for advice. HR recommends profiling Kerri, looking in particular at her sources of motivation which currently appear to be non-existent.

Kerri agrees to complete a motivation questionnaire to see how best her boredom can be dealt with. The **SHL Motivation Questionnaire (MQ)** is chosen because it may hold the key to what would be the best next steps.

This questionnaire measures 18 dimensions of an individual's motivation, and provides a comprehensive understanding of those situations which increase and reduce their motivation. It also helps to determine how long and under what circumstances effort will be maintained.

TESTING FOR PERSONAL DEVELOPMENT

MOTIVATION QUESTIONNAIRE

SHL MOTIVATION QUESTIONNAIRE (MQ) 18 DIMENSIONS

Some people may be motivated by **energy and dynamism** – the energy with which an individual approaches tasks:

1. Level of activity – how energy is invested
2. Achievement – need to achieve targets, competition
3. Competition – attempt to out do others
4. Fear of failure – prospect of failure, spears activity
5. Power – need to exercise authority
6. Immersion – need to feel involved
7. Commercial outlook – wants to create wealth and profits

Some people may be motivated by **synergy** – feeling comfortable and at ease with the work environment:

1. Affiliation – thrives on meeting people and team work
2. Recognition – likes good work to be noticed
3. Personal principles – wishing to operate in an ethical manner
4. Ease and security – need to feel secure about their job
5. Personal growth – work should provide opportunities for development

MOTIVATION QUESTIONNAIRE

SHL MOTIVATION QUESTIONNAIRE (MQ) 18 DIMENSIONS

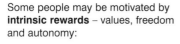

Some people may be motivated by **intrinsic rewards** – values, freedom and autonomy:

1. Interest – values, stimulating or creative work
2. Flexibility – favours a fluid environment without structure
3. Autonomy – need to work independently, organise self

Some people may be motivated by **extrinsic rewards** – loads of money:

1. Material reward – links salary and income to success
2. Progression – needs an upwards career path
3. Status – concerned with position, status and the respect they bring

TESTING FOR PERSONAL DEVELOPMENT

MOTIVATION QUESTIONNAIRE

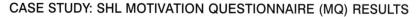

CASE STUDY: SHL MOTIVATION QUESTIONNAIRE (MQ) RESULTS

During the feedback session, it is evident that Kerri has high scores in the following areas:

- **Achievement and competition** – the need to reach targets as well as work in a competitive environment
- **Fear of failure**
- **Power, immersion and commercial outlook**

It is clear that Kerri has a high level of energy and dynamism, possibly too much for the mundane nature of the role. In discussion with the HR manager, they agree that Kerri is not suited to her current role and, with the agreement of her boss, they decide to transfer her into retail sales. In such a post she can use her energy more appropriately dealing directly with customers, meeting targets and satisfying her need for achievement, immersion and commercial activity. Above all, she will be able to see quite clearly that she is not failing.

Without use of the questionnaire to identify more satisfying areas of work, it is likely that Kerri would have left in search of 'less boring' work or taken up negative attitudes and become disruptive. Either way, the bank would have lost a potentially highly talented performer.

PERSONALITY TESTS

We move on to look at personality tests to find the best ways of helping others develop. We have already discussed, in the *Testing for Selection* chapter, the background to personality tests and how difficult it can be to select a test from the hundreds flooding the market place. This may put people off. It is, however, well worth making the effort to assist individuals to reach an understanding of their unique personality.

We have chosen to illustrate a foundation test, one with an acclaimed pedigree of research reliability and validity and of particular use in a personal development and change context.

TESTING FOR PERSONAL DEVELOPMENT

PERSONALITY TESTS

CASE STUDY: ECCOS TEST

Sunita works successfully in a lively sales operation, but has recently married, is starting a family and wishes to explore careers where she can develop her people skills in an environment with young children, so that she can integrate family life more closely with her work and her personality. She is thinking about becoming a nursery teacher. Sunita wishes to understand how she can make this career change through a personal development process. She visits a trained counsellor who suggests using a personality questionnaire as a start.

The personality test chosen has been developed from the **Eysenck Personality Questionnaire**. Hans Eysenck first began developing this test as long ago as 1952 while working at the Maudsley Hospital in London. Dr Barry Cripps and Dr Mark Cook, together with Dr Sybil Eysenck, have produced **ECCOS, The Eysenck, Cripps, Cook, Occupational Scales**, measuring seven aspects of personality. **ECCOS** has three features which distinguish it from most other personality questionnaires: links to psychology in general, very extensive cross-cultural research making it truly pan-cultural and a direct application into the world of work.

Used with kind permission of Eysenck, Cripps, Cook Occupational Scales (2007) www.eccos.co.uk

TESTING FOR PERSONAL DEVELOPMENT

PERSONALITY TESTS

SEVEN SCALES OF ECCOS

The seven scales are as follows:

1. **Tender-minded:** sociable and caring for people –
   Tough-minded: sometimes alone and not overly concerned with people.
2. **Introvert:** quiet, reliable, doesn't make a fuss –
   Extravert: very sociable, outgoing, seeks stimulation and change.
3. **Stable:** relaxed, calm and controlled –
   Anxious: worries overly about things, may lose control.
4. **Low Impulsive:** looks ahead at consequences –
   Impulsive: may not consider consequences.
5. **Low Venturesome:** cautious, unlikely to take risks –
   Venturesome: true risk-taking behaviour.
6. **Low Empathy:** may not see other person point of view or perspective –
   Empathy: able to understand another person perspective and put self in their shoes.
7. **Social Desirability:** (a faking detector) this is a built in scale which detects whether the test taker has been open and honest with their responses to the test questions, or is seeking perfection.

Used with kind permission of Eysenck, Cripps, Cook Occupational Scales (2007) www.eccos.co.uk

TESTING FOR PERSONAL DEVELOPMENT

PERSONALITY TESTS
CASE STUDY: ECCOS

Sunita completes the personality test and her results are displayed below:

SUNITA'S SCORES

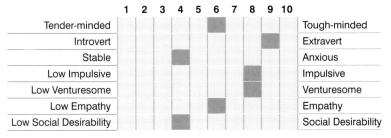

	1	2	3	4	5	6	7	8	9	10	
Tender-minded						■					Tough-minded
Introvert									■		Extravert
Stable				■							Anxious
Low Impulsive								■			Impulsive
Low Venturesome								■			Venturesome
Low Empathy						■					Empathy
Low Social Desirability				■							Social Desirability

Used with kind permission of Eysenck, Cripps, Cook Occupational Scales (2007) www.eccos.co.uk

PERSONALITY TESTS

CASE STUDY: ECCOS RESULTS

Sunita reports herself in the middle (**6**) of the Tough- Tender-minded scale, indicating a level of interest in others, and an ability to take people or leave them. Her score of **9** for Extravert reflects her bubbly, fairly assertive temperament, ready to accept the changes in development she is choosing.

Her score of **4** for Stable will see her taking a fairly calm, even tempered, flexible approach, reasonably able to accept the stresses of teaching. Sunita shows a typical level of empathy (**6**), usually able to see others' points of view and read their feelings. At **4** on the Social Desirability scale, she indicates that she has answered honestly and openly and not tried to fake her results.

Sunita and her counsellor reason that this personality profile can help her positively in her objective of becoming a teacher (though she may need to rein in her impulsiveness for reality checks at times).

The technique of using a personality test in counselling for personal development is a powerful way of 'opening up' the client and uncovering personality trait data of use in helping the client move in new directions.

Used with kind permission of Eysenck, Cripps, Cook Occupational Scales (2007) www.eccos.co.uk

EI ABILITY TEST

CASE STUDY: MSCEIT

We have already mentioned emotional intelligence in the section on Organisational Development. The following test looks at EI from a completely different perspective.

Andrew is an operations manager for a major organisation. He was informed by his boss that he and his team were going to be relocated from the buzz of the square mile in the heart of the City of London to a less desirable area south of the River Thames.

The move was not without its problems, particularly when it came to uprooting staff from the trendy bars and restaurants they had become attached to. Andrew listened to his team's complaints and understood their feelings very well indeed. However, as each problem was resolved another complaint came up. After a while this had a noticeable effect on the productivity of the group. At this point, Andrew was referred for executive coaching to help him resolve the issues around managing his people.

The coach asked Andrew to complete the **Mayer Salovey Caruso Emotional Intelligence Test (MSCEIT)**, developed by Peter Salovey, John Mayer and David Caruso.

EI ABILITY TEST

THE MSCEIT EMOTIONAL INTELLIGENCE TEST

The MSCEIT test is based on an ability model of emotional intelligence designed to assess the potential (or capacity) for emotionally intelligent behaviour. It takes a very different approach from many of the other psychometric instruments in this pocketbook.

The test authors state that their model defines emotional intelligence as the ability to reason with, and about emotions, and that for optimal performance to take place thinking and feeling have to work together in harmony.

The MSCEIT model consists of the following **Emotional Blueprint**:

1. Identifying Emotions: *What emotions are you, and others, experiencing?*
2. Using Emotions: *How are these emotions directing attention and influencing thinking?*
3. Understanding Emotions: *What caused these emotions and how might they change?*
4. Managing Emotions: *What emotional strategies best address the problem?*

TESTING FOR PERSONAL DEVELOPMENT

EI ABILITY TEST

THE MSCEIT EMOTIONAL INTELLIGENCE TEST

How we handle our emotions, whether in one to one situations, in a team, or in the boardroom is very important to an individual's success in the workplace.

David Caruso, one of the authors of the MSCEIT quotes directly:

"You can ask a client to provide a self-estimate of their emotional abilities, and they will gladly comply with your request. The problem is that these confident self-assessments are often at times dead wrong. Because the MSCEIT is like an objective test, an IQ test for emotions, many people are surprised and sometimes upset by their results. Some clients have completely dismissed the entire notion of EI, as they struggle with their assessment results. That's when we examine their scores, and note, with a sense of irony, very low scores on their ability to effectively manage emotions."
David Caruso (Mayer, Salovey & Caruso Emotional Intelligence Test - 2007)

EI ABILITY TEST

EXAMPLE OF THE MSCEIT

Here is an example of the MSCEIT type items in the questionnaire. See what responses you might come up with yourself:

Q1. Perceiving Emotions

What emotions are expressed by this face?

	Low				High
Happiness	1	2	3	4	5
Fear	1	2	3	4	5

Answer: Happiness, surely, but the ratings will vary. Ours was 4!

TESTING FOR PERSONAL DEVELOPMENT

EI ABILITY TEST

EXAMPLE OF THE MSCEIT

Q2. Using emotions

How helpful would each of these feelings be when proofing a budget
for the last time before it is submitted in a contract proposal?

	Not helpful				Very helpful
a. Some tension	1	2	3	4	5
b. Joy	1	2	3	4	5
c. Excitement	1	2	3	4	5

Answer: We answered tension 3, joy 1 and excitement 2.

TESTING FOR PERSONAL DEVELOPMENT

EI ABILITY TEST

EXAMPLE OF THE MSCEIT

Q3. Understanding emotions

A feeling of contempt most closely combines the emotions of (select one):

a. Surprise and anger

b. Anger and fear

c. Anxiety and fear

d. Disgust and anger

e. Hatred and guilt

Answer: We answered d. as the closest, because disgust seems to fit but not necessarily anger.

TESTING FOR PERSONAL DEVELOPMENT

EI ABILITY TEST

EXAMPLE OF THE MSCEIT

Q4. Managing emotions

A manager received sad news. He wants to feel happy before attending an important client meeting. How helpful is each of these in getting him to feel happy:

	Not helpful				Very helpful
Listen to sad music to calm down	1	2	3	4	5
Review his accomplishments	1	2	3	4	5
Sit alone in his office	1	2	3	4	5

Answer: We leave you to make your own mind up for this question!

EI ABILITY TEST

CASE STUDY: MSCEIT RESULTS

In Andrew's case the results provided confirmation and clarification of the issues involved in his management skills. The chart shows that he was fairly competent at **perceiving** (Perceiving Emotions) how his staff felt, and was extremely skilled at **understanding** why they felt as they did and how their feelings changed from day to day (Understanding Emotions). However, he was not integrating this emotional information into his decision making. Instead of **engaging** with the emotions (Using & Managing) he blocked them out.

Improve / Consider Developing / Competent / Skilled / Expert

Perceiving Emotions
Using Emotions
Understanding Emotions
Managing Emotions

The MSCEIT results provided Andrew with both the insight and the process by which he could enhance his management style; helping him use his own emotions more when talking with his people, eg *'Well I don't want to move either, but I'm sure that once I've solved my journey problems, working in the new building will be much more peaceful'*.

Andrew received coaching to develop the way he managed his own emotions when making decisions, eg working with uncertainty in a less predictable environment.

TESTING FOR CAREER COUNSELLING

TESTING FOR CAREER COUNSELLING

INTERESTS & VALUES INVENTORIES

So far we have discussed how aptitude, personality and emotional intelligence tests help the individual develop a heightened self-awareness. We will now highlight how using a career interests and values inventory can help an individual focus on areas for career exploration. Psychometric tests can give us an informed perspective on our strengths and weaknesses, allowing us to focus on any new skills needed.

As part of an in-depth careers interview it is beneficial to use a **combination** of different tests, allowing greater self-understanding of the individual, eg:

- **Aptitude tests** which measure your ability for particular types of activity or ways of thinking, and identify any special talent for a certain type of job, eg numerical aptitude for accountancy
- **Personality tests** designed to find out how you might react in certain situations
- **Emotional Intelligence tests** which measure certain behaviours relating to how you manage your own emotions and those of others around you
- **Interests and Values Inventories** which help with an individual's self perceptions and career aspirations. They tend to look at areas such as: preferred working style, career development and career direction

> 'What is necessary to change a person is to change his awareness of himself'
> **Abraham Maslow**

INTERESTS & VALUES INVENTORIES

CASE STUDY: STRONG INTEREST INVENTORY® (SII) TOOL

Samantha, who was 24, had worked in various casual jobs in pubs and restaurants since leaving school. She was unhappy and very confused about what type of job she would be most suited to. She made an appointment to see a qualified career consultant who was licensed to administer a range of psychometric tests and would be able to aid her in exploring different career options.

As part of Samantha's career exploration she was asked to complete the **Strong Interest Inventory® (SII) tool**. The inventory, originally developed in the 1920s and subsequently revised, is used worldwide. It is backed up by decades of research with people who are satisfied in their careers. The current version is based on the ideas of John Holland.

The best way to use Interest Inventories is as a guide to possibilities only. We cannot emphasise enough how important it is to research any career interests, speak to someone already doing that job to see if it is really what you want to do, and where possible undertake work experience or work shadowing. Research shows that people are most productive in work that they enjoy doing.

Strong Interest Inventory is a registered trademark of CPP, Inc. Used with permission

TESTING FOR CAREER COUNSELLING

INTERESTS & VALUES INVENTORIES

CAREER INTEREST INVENTORIES

Most of us have limited knowledge of the range of jobs that exist even within our own occupational arena. This is why using an Interest Inventory is of value to those who already have some idea of where they want to work as well as to individuals who do not know where to start.

Career Interest Inventories encourage people to think about the world of work and the areas that interest them the most. For instance they:

- Identify career options consistent with interests
- Highlight career options that haven't been considered
- Choose appropriate education and training routes relevant to interests
- Help maintain a balance between work and leisure activities
- Understand a preferred learning environment
- Learn about preferences for leadership, risk taking, and teamwork
- Use interests in shaping career directions
- Decide on a work oriented focus for the future
- Provide an insight into aspects of the world of work

TESTING FOR CAREER COUNSELLING.

INTERESTS & VALUES INVENTORIES
STRONG INTEREST INVENTORY® (SII) TOOL

John Holland's (1959) model of fit between work environments and the individual provides a unifying framework or model of six occupational themes into which most jobs fit. The newly revised Strong Interest Inventory® tool puts focus on business and technology careers.

Holland's six occupational themes

Theme	Interests	Work activities
Realistic	Mechanical, tools, outdoors	Operating equipment, using tools, building, repairing
Investigative	Science, theories, ideas, data	Lab work, problem solving, researching, analysing
Artistic	Self-expression, art appreciation	Composing music, drama, writing, creating visual art, cooking

Continued →

Strong Interest Inventory is a registered trademark of CPP, Inc. Used with permission

TESTING FOR CAREER COUNSELLING.

INTERESTS & VALUES INVENTORIES

STRONG INTEREST INVENTORY® (SII) TOOL

Holland's six occupational themes (continued)

Theme	Interests	Work activities
Social	People, teamwork, helping others, community service	Teaching, explaining, instructing, care giving
Enterprising	Business, politics, leadership, influence	Selling, persuading, managing
Conventional	Organisation, data, finance	Setting up procedures, organising, processing data

Strong Interest Inventory is a registered trademark of CPP, Inc. Used with permission

INTERESTS & VALUES INVENTORIES

CASE STUDY: STRONG INTEREST INVENTORY® (SII) TOOL RESULTS

Having completed the inventory, Samantha's Strong Interest Career themes came out (in order of strength) as:

1. **Social** – people oriented, teamworker, helping, teaching, caring for others.
2. **Conventional** – organisation, data management, setting up procedures, keeping records.

Her top occupational preferences, as indicated by the SII, were nursing and social care.

It became clear during the feedback session, and from her work history, that Samantha was very sociable and outgoing. Meeting and helping others was something she really enjoyed. However, the social side was no longer enough for her: she had begun to realise that a career was important. The next issue to explore was her values.

The values that we each hold influence how we deal with everyday tasks both inside and outside the workplace. Exploring an individual's values in a development, teambuilding or career counselling situation can lead to an understanding and resolution of problem areas, the development of stronger teams and the clarification of career goals. The SPV questionnaire (see next page) was used to explore Samantha's values, both personally and interpersonally.

Strong Interest Inventory is a registered trademark of CPP, Inc. Used with permission

INTERESTS & VALUES INVENTORIES

GORDON'S SURVEYS OF PERSONAL & INTERPERSONAL VALUES (SPV & SIV)

Survey of Personal Values (SPV)

Leonard V Gordon started research into personality in 1953, before moving on to look at the values we hold that influence how we deal with everyday tasks and people both inside and outside the workplace. Exploring an individual's values in a counselling situation can lead to an understanding and resolution of problem areas like the clarification of life or career goals.

The SPV is designed to measure certain critical values that help determine the manner in which individuals cope with the problems of everyday living:

1. **Practical mindedness** – likes practical things, material – and economically – minded.
2. **Achievement** – values growth, accomplishment, enjoys challenge and effort.
3. **Variety** – prefers a range of activity, dislikes routine, prefers new experiences.
4. **Decisiveness** – values and sticks to own opinions, likes thinking through decisions.
5. **Orderliness** – prefers organisation, routine and schedules.
6. **Goal orientation** – prefers clear objectives and seeing tasks to completion.

INTERESTS & VALUES INVENTORIES

GORDON'S SURVEYS OF PERSONAL & INTERPERSONAL VALUES (SPV & SIV)

Survey of Interpersonal Values (SIV)

The SIV is designed to measure certain values involving the individual's personal, social, marital and occupational adjustment:

1. **Support** – values kindness, encouragement and consideration from others.
2. **Conformity** – doing the correct thing, following regulation.
3. **Recognition** – being looked up to, considered important, admired.
4. **Independence** – doing what one wants, making own decisions.
5. **Benevolence** – doing things for others, sharing, helping those in need.
6. **Leadership** – being in charge, having authority, power.

TESTING FOR CAREER COUNSELLING

INTERESTS & VALUES INVENTORIES

GORDON'S SURVEYS OF PERSONAL
& INTERPERSONAL VALUES (SPV & SIV)

By using the Gordon Survey of Personal and Interpersonal Values questionnaire Samantha was helped to delve deeper into her individual value system. She found that she:

- Valued growth and challenge and an occupation that involved variety
- Valued recognition and the need to feel in charge

This extra self-understanding was discussed with her career counsellor. The job areas of nursing and social work were highlighted as areas for further investigation and research. Training would be required in both these roles.

Following career counselling it was strongly recommended that she also spoke to people already working in those jobs and to tutors about the course content and whether she had the correct qualifications. The outcome was that Samantha decided to explore nursing as a career.

USEFUL INFORMATION

TESTING ONLINE

Online psychometric test administration is proving to be a very popular choice for assessing individuals and nowadays tends to be preferred to paper and pencil based test administration.

For multinational organisations that may wish to test individuals in different countries in, say, the space of an afternoon, the fact that tests can be completed over the internet makes online testing of enormous practical benefit. In addition, many tests are now available in multiple languages (eg the Expert Testing System used by Thomas International (DISC) is available in over 50 languages), making testing online very accessible to different cultures across different continents.

However, there are advantages and disadvantages to testing online which the test user needs to be made aware of.

TESTING ONLINE

ADVANTAGES

The advantages of online testing for both test takers and test users are:

- **Cost effective** – cuts out the assessment centre where test takers would normally be called to sit a paper and pencil test. Instead the individual can complete the test from their own laptop or computer
- **Secure** – the test taker is provided, by the test administrator, with a confidential login and password. This directs the test taker to a secure, online assessment site, owned by the test distributor
- **More flexible** – test takers can complete an array of tests around the globe. Online assessment site test access is normally available 7 days a week, 24 hours a day
- **No paper** – there is no need to carry large amounts of paperwork with you
- **Quick turnaround** – when the test taker has completed an online test the administrator will be notified, normally via email. The test administrator then accesses the online assessment site, locates the test taker's report and scores it electronically. The report is produced in a PDF format in a matter of seconds. Alternatively, scoring can be done by a scoring bureau which then forwards the scored report to the test administrator

TESTING ONLINE

DISADVANTAGES

- **Verification** of test taker – are they who they say they are?
- **Distractions** – when the test administrator sends instructions, it is beneficial to provide the test taker with some guidelines on appropriate times to complete the test, ie free from other distractions and with sufficient time available to answer as accurately as possible. They should choose a time when they are not too stressed or tired, not influenced by alcohol, and definitely not asking friends for help: 'Er Geoff ...do you think this is me?'
- **Ability tests** – the test taker may cheat, using the internet for help in formulating answers
- **Feedback** – It is always good practice to provide feedback. There is nothing worse than for the test taker to complete an assessment and then just receive, by email, a PDF electronically scored report, produced by an Expert System with no other feedback, particularly when the results are not that flattering, or the test taker is thinking: 'this isn't me!' Face to face feedback is best but if this is not possible, telephone or video conferencing are acceptable alternatives
- **Language interpretation** – misunderstandings of translation can occur because there is nobody to verify translation
- **First language** – tests should be in the test taker's native language to avoid language misinterpretation

USEFUL INFORMATION

GOOD PRACTICE

It is important that the test administration should follow a standardised procedure whether we are measuring personality, ability, aptitudes, motivation or vocational interests. Then we can assume that if all the test takers have been treated similarly, any variation in scores will be within the people and not in the test conditions.

Short-term environmental factors that can affect and possibly reduce test performance are:

- Room lighting
- Room temperature
- Noise
- Distractions
- Time of day
- Attitude of test administrator
- Illness on the day

Test users **can** control the above.

GOOD PRACTICE

Long-term environmental factors that can affect and possibly reduce test performance are:

- Parental influence, upbringing
- Quality of education
- Cultural background
- Illness or disability

Test users **cannot** control the above but may be aware of how they may affect test results.

STANDARDS IN TESTING, TRAINING & CERTIFICATION

The British Psychological Society has devised a certification scheme to train people in the proper use of occupational tests. The Certificates of Competence in Occupational Testing (Levels A/B/B+/Full) are delivered by assessors who must be chartered psychologists. The main benefits of the scheme are that it provides:

- A clear specification of what the potential test user needs to know and be able to do, to use tests properly
- Access to most ability and aptitude tests, interest inventories and career guidance materials
- Evidence of qualifications which should be 'transferable' between various providers of training in testing and between various publishers and other suppliers of test materials

- A form of national certification of competence in occupational testing which employers will be encouraged to recognise for the proper use of psychological testing within their organisations. If employers stipulate that testing may only be carried out by or under the direction of suitably qualified people, professional standards in testing should improve

A code of good practice is available from the Psychological Testing Centre www.psychtesting.org.uk

CONCLUSION

We have introduced the reader to psychometric testing as generally applied in the workplace. Starting with selection testing, we have then moved on to show how testing can also be useful in developing organisations, teams and individuals. Testing has been shown to be of prime importance in career counselling, mainly to direct personality and ability strengths towards choosing a career compatible with personality traits, values and aspirations. Job satisfaction is a powerful ingredient in successful performance and well-being in the workplace.

We recommend that organisations write a policy for good practice in occupational testing and follow guidelines recommended by the British Psychological Society Psychological Test Centre.

The authors would like to stress that the choice of tests and the opinions in this book are their own. We recommend that training in test use is undertaken as a first step, after advice about testing has been sought from experienced psychologists or trained test users.

FURTHER READING & REFERENCES

Bar-On EQ-i
Multi-Health Systems Inc, Toronto, Canada and the
United Kingdom www.mhs.com
Dr Reuven Bar-On www.reuvenbaron.org

Belbin Team Roles,
Belbin Associates, Cambridge, United Kingdom
www.belbin.com

Certificates of Competence (Level A & B) in
Occupational Testing www.psychtesting.org.uk

ECCOS
(Eysenck, Cripps, Cook Occupational Scales):
A User's Guide, Cook M. and Cripps B.D. 2007
www.eccos.co.uk

EQ 360 Multi-Rater Feedback
Multi-Health Systems Inc, Toronto, Canada and the
United Kingdom www.mhs.com

General Ability Tests (GAT2)
ASE Human Capital Consulting, London
www.ase-solutions.co.uk

Gordon's SPV & SIV
ASE Human Capital Consulting, London
www.ase-solutions.co.uk

Mayer, Salovey, Caruso Emotional Intelligence Tool
Multi-Health Systems Inc, Toronto, Canada and the
United Kingdom www.mhs.com

Myers-Briggs Type Indicator®
Oxford Psychologists Press (OPP) Oxford, United
Kingdom www.opp.eu.com and Consulting
Psychologists Press (CPP) Palo Alto, California
www.cpp.com

Personal Profile Analysis (PPA)
Thomas International of Marlow, UK.
www.thomasinternational.net

SHL Motivational Questionnaire
SHL Group Ltd. SHL is a registered trade mark of
SHL Group Ltd www.shl.com

FURTHER READING & REFERENCES

Strong Interest Inventory® (SII) (newly revised) Consulting Psychologists Press (CPP) Palo Alto, California www.cpp.com

Saville Consulting Wave®
www.savilleconsulting.com MacIver R, Saville P, Kurz R, Mitchener A, Mariscal K, Parry G, Becker S, Saville W, O'Connor K, Patterson R & Oxley H (2006). *Making Waves – Saville Consulting Wave Styles questionnaires. Selection & Development Review,* 22 (2), pp 17-23.

W-GCTA
Watson G. and Glaser M. (2002) Watson-Glaser Critical Thinking Appraisal UK Edition. The Psychological Corporation, London. www.harcourt-uk.com

Quality of Working Life Questionnaire
ASE Human Capital Consulting, London www.ase-solutions.co.uk

16PF Oxford Psychologists Press (OPP) Oxford, United Kingdom www.opp.eu.com

BOOKS AND JOURNALS

Emotional Intelligence, Goleman D, Bantam Books, 1995

The EQ Edge, Emotional Intelligence and Your Success, Stein S.J (Ph.D) and Howard E.B (M.D), Jossey-Bass 2000 and 2006 revised, www.mhs.com

Working with Emotional Intelligence, Goleman D, Bloomsbury Publishing, 1998

Psychological Assessment in the Workplace – A Manager's Guide, Cook M. and Cripps B.D, John Wiley & Sons, 2005

A Theory of Vocational Choice, Holland J.L, Journal of Counselling Psychology,1959, spr, vol 6 (1) 35-45

Emotions of Normal People, Marston W.M, Routledge, 2002

About the Authors

Dr Barry Cripps

Dr Barry Cripps is a chartered occupational psychologist independently consulting in industry, business, higher education and sport. His interests are in executive coaching, organisational learning, development and assessment. He has served as a main board Director of Training, is an external examiner in HR to top ranking business schools, advisor to the CIPD and is verifier of test competence in the British Psychological Society. Barry practises from his rooms in Dartington, Devon.

Contact   Website: www.performance-psychology.com
E-mail: drbarrycripps@btinternet.com

Dorothy Spry

Dorothy Spry is a business psychologist who has worked with a wide range of clients in both the public and private sectors. Her interests are in building staff and customer loyalty training, international online psychometric test scoring and interpretation, career counselling and emotional intelligence EQ-i & EQ360 accreditation training and licensing. Dorothy is a foundation trainer for ECCOS. She is also a career guidance skills assessor and works in both the United Kingdom and internationally where she runs a variety of self-awareness raising workshops. She also lectures in Romania, Dubai, Holland and New York. Dorothy is a National Training Award winner of the UK's premier award for training and development (2007).

Contact   Website: www.careerperformance.co.uk
E-mail: dorothy@careerperformance.co.uk

ORDER FORM

Your details

Name _____

Position _____

Company _____

Address _____

_____

_____

Telephone _____

Fax _____

E-mail _____

VAT No. (EC companies) _____

Your Order Ref _____

Please send me:

			No. copies
The	Psychometric Testing	Pocketbook	
The	_____	Pocketbook	
The	_____	Pocketbook	
The	_____	Pocketbook	

Order by Post

**MANAGEMENT
POCKETBOOKS LTD**
LAUREL HOUSE, STATION APPROACH,
ALRESFORD, HAMPSHIRE SO24 9JH UK

Order by Phone, Fax or Internet
Telephone: +44 (0)1962 735573
Facsimile: +44 (0)1962 733637
E-mail: sales@pocketbook.co.uk
Web: www.pocketbook.co.uk

Customers in USA should contact:
Management Pocketbooks
2427 Bond Street, University Park, IL 60466
Telephone: 866 620 6944   Facsimile: 708 534 7803
E-mail: mp.orders@ware-pak.com
Web: www.managementpocketbooks.com